LEARNING FRENCH IS FUN AND EASY!

Language Learning 4th Grade | Children's Foreign Language Books

Copyright 2018

Let's learn
the French
language!

Let's talk
in French!

Let's learn more words in French!

GREETINGS IN FRENCH

Salut

(sah-lew)

Hi / Bye

Bonjour

(boh(n)-zhoor)

Hello

Bonsoir

(boh(n)-swahr)

Hello (after 7pm)

Bonne soirée

(bohn swah-ray)

Good evening

Enchanté

(ahn-shant-ay)

pleased to meet you
(to a male)

Quoi de neuf?

(kwah duh nuhf)

What's up?

Enchantée

(ahn-shant-ay)

pleased to meet you
(to a female)

Bienvenue

bee-ehn veh-noo

Welcome

Santé

(sahn-tay)

Cheers

HOW TO BID FAREWELL IN FRENCH

À tout à l'heure

(ah too-tah luhr)

See you (later today)

À la prochaine

(ah lah proh-shehn)

See you (tomorrow)

À bientôt

(ah byuha(n)-toh)

See you soon

À plus tard

(ah plew tahr)

See you later

Ciao

(chow)

Bye

Bonne journée

(bohn zhoor-nay)

Have a nice day

Au revoir

(oh ruh-vwahr)

Good-bye

Bonne chance

(bohn shahnce)

Good luck

Bonne nuit

(bohn nooee)

Good night

POLITE EXPRESSIONS IN FRENCH

À demain

(ah duh-ma(n))

See you tomorrow

À vos souhaits

(ah voh soo-eht)

Bless you

Let's learn more words in French!

Pas grand-chose

(pah grah(n) shohz)

Not much

Merci

(mehr-see)

Thank you

Merci beaucoup

(mehr-see bo-koo)

Thank you very much

De rien

(deh ree-en)

You're welcome

Body parts
in French!

face | visage

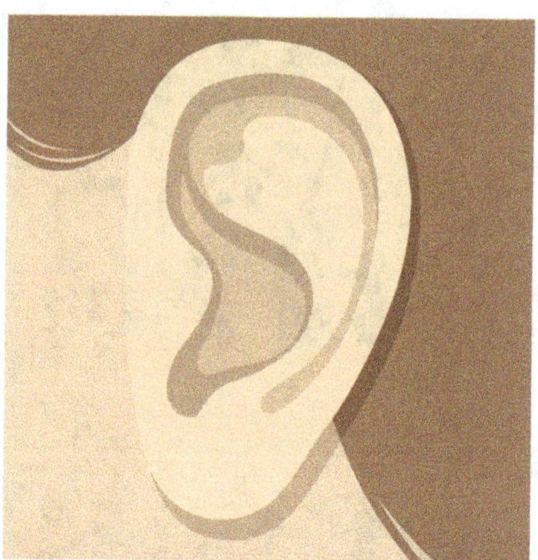

ear | oreille

teeth | les dents

nose | nez

hair | cheveux

neck | cou

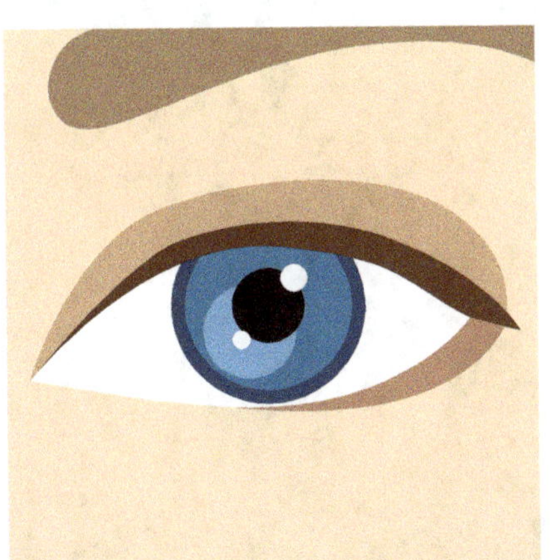

eye | œil

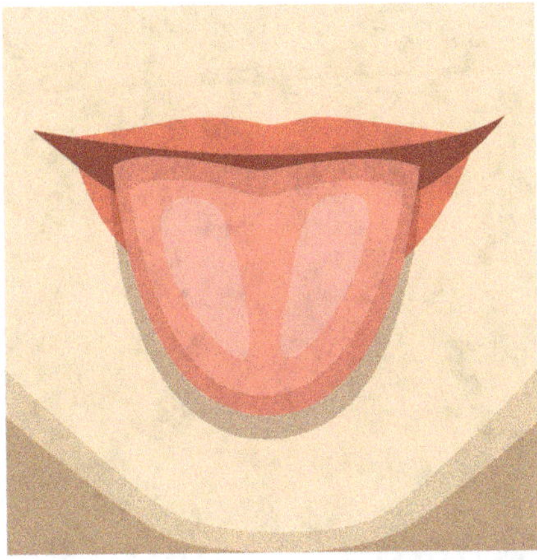

tongue | langue

| lips | lèvres |

| forehead | front |

cheek | joue

mouth | bouche

chin | menton

eyebrow | sourcil

head | tête

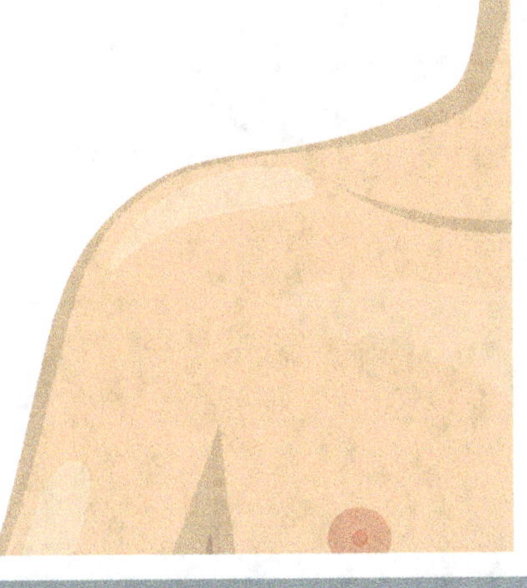

shoulder | épaule

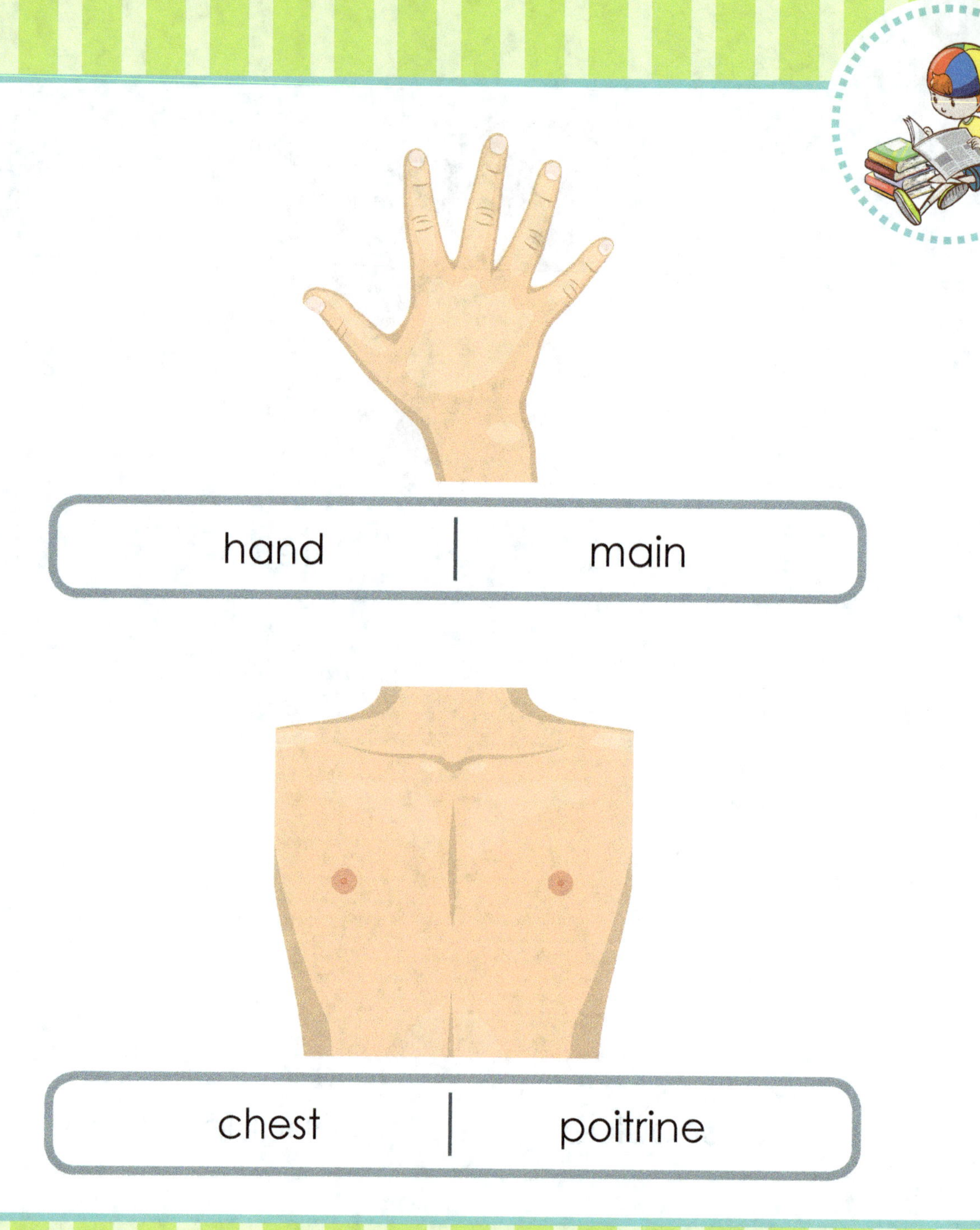

hand | main

chest | poitrine

back | arrière
thumb | pouce

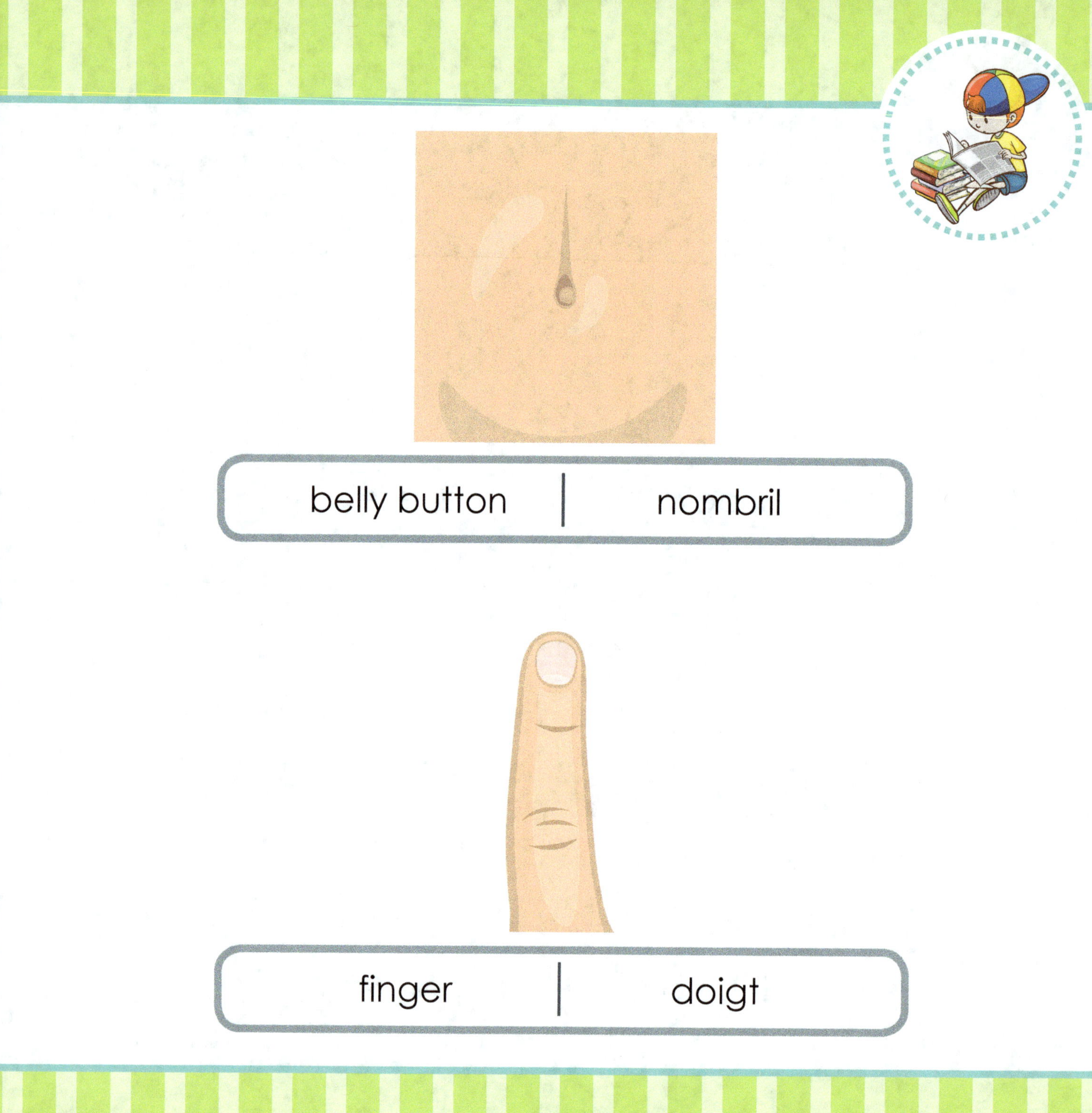

belly button | nombril
finger | doigt

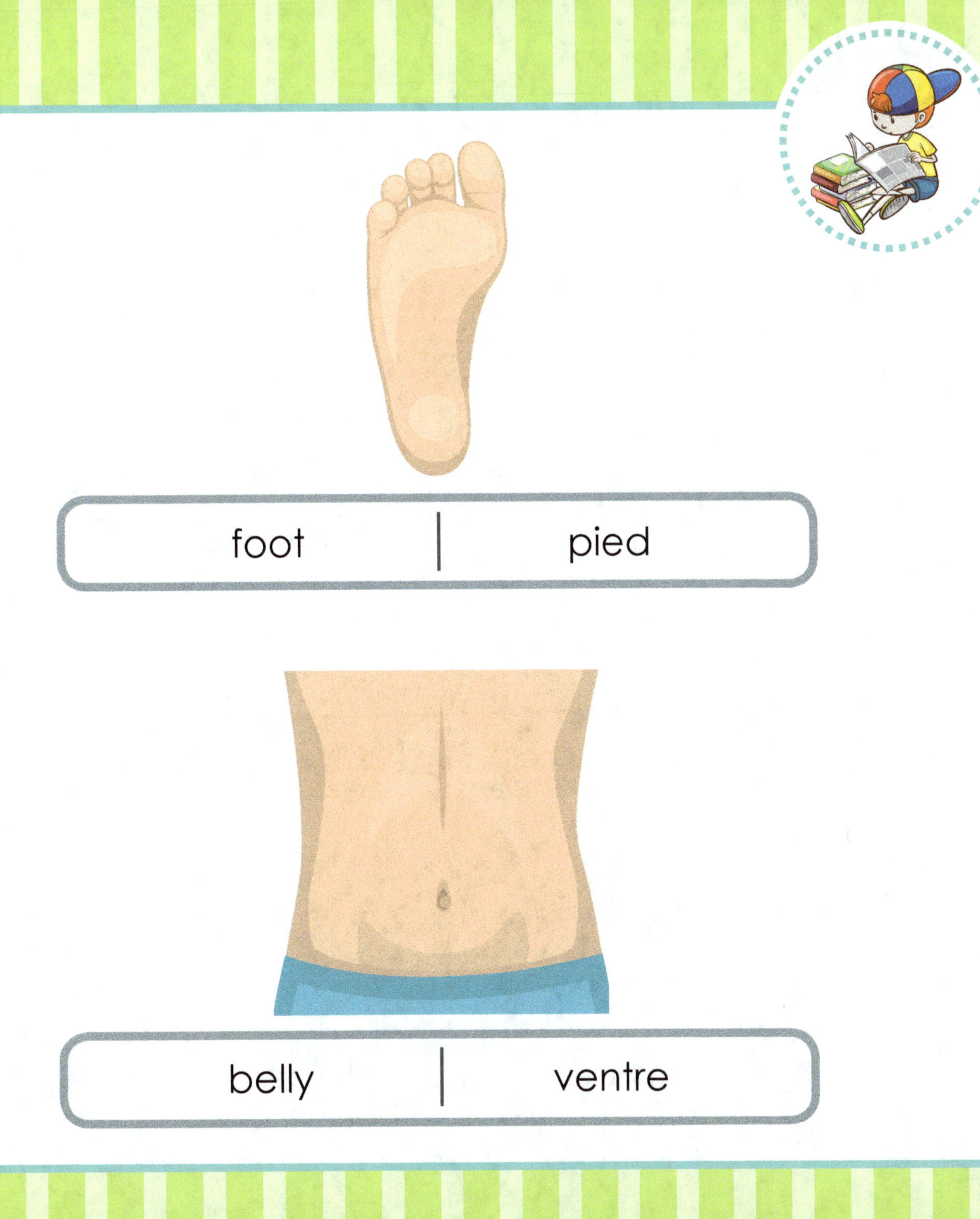

foot | pied
belly | ventre

leg | jambe
knee | le genou

arm | bras
ankle | cheville

Clothes
in French!

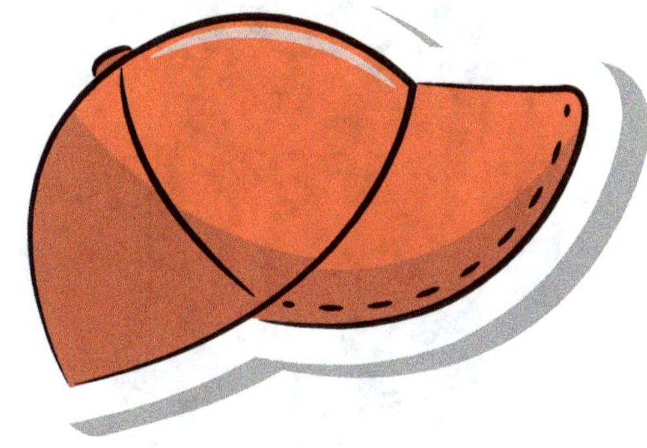

| une casquette | a cap |

| un tee-shirt | a t-shirt |

un sweat | a sweatshirt

un pantalon | pants

une jupe | a skirt

des chaussettes | socks

| des chaussures | shoes |

| Un slip | underwear |

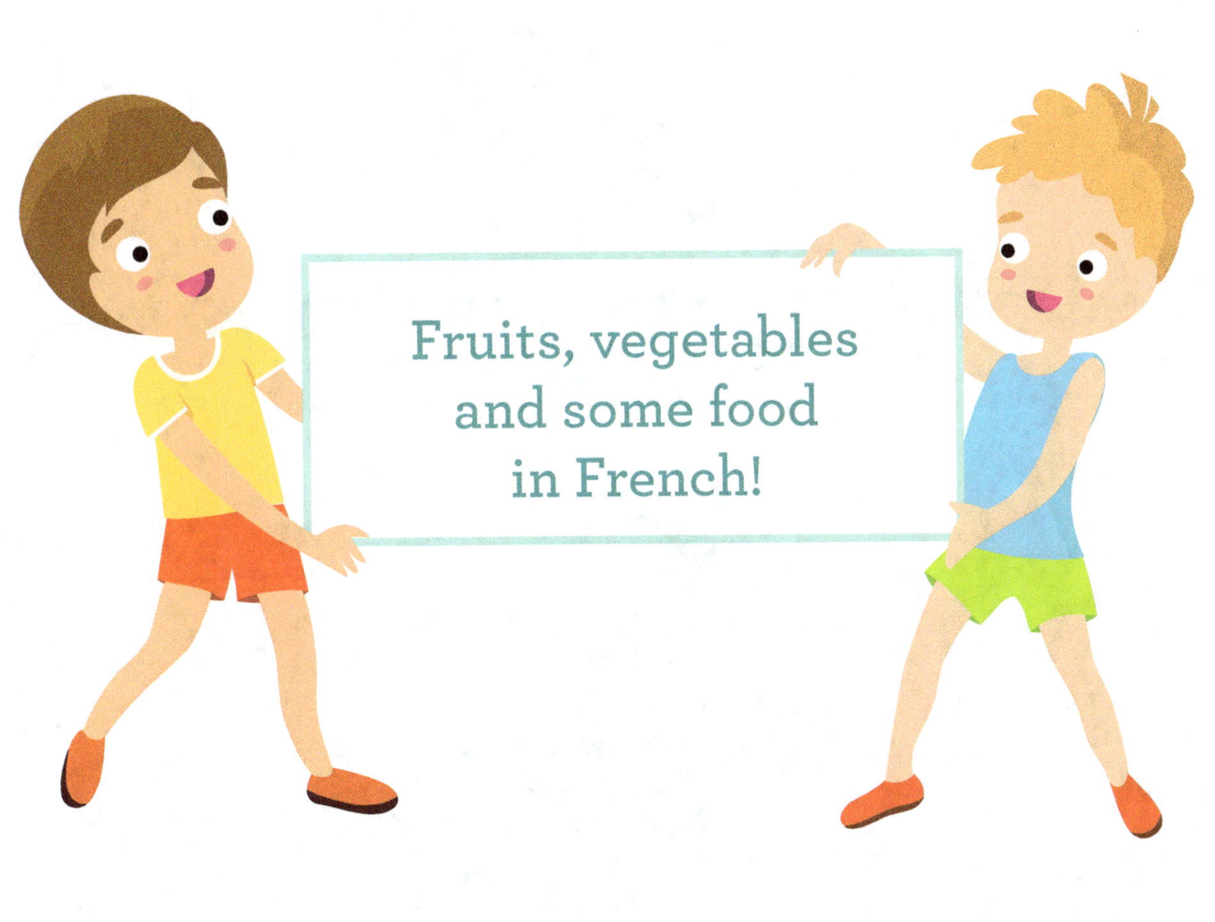

Fruits, vegetables
and some food
in French!

bananas | bananes

apple | pomme

| pear | poire |

| orange | orange |

pomegranate | grenade

pineapple | ananas

grapes | les raisins

lemon | citron

avocado	avocat

kiwifruit	kiwis

| tomato | tomate |

| eggplant | aubergine |

garlic | ail

bell pepper | poivron

onion	oignon

pumpkin	citrouille

mushroom | champignon

cabbage | chou

corn | blé

carrots | carottes

peas | pois

cucumber | concombre

meat | viande

milk | lait

| egg | oeuf |

| bread | pain |

Short
Quiz!

Write the french translation of each word below.

ENGLISH	FRENCH
Good night	____________________
Hello	____________________
Thank you	____________________
Good luck	____________________
Welcome	____________________

Write the french translation of each word below.

ENGLISH	FRENCH
face	_ _ _ _ _ _ _ _ _ _ _ _
nose	_ _ _ _ _ _ _ _ _ _ _ _
hair	_ _ _ _ _ _ _ _ _ _ _ _
eye	_ _ _ _ _ _ _ _ _ _ _ _
teeth	_ _ _ _ _ _ _ _ _ _ _ _

Write the french translation of each word below.

ENGLISH	FRENCH
ear	____________________
head	____________________
chin	____________________
hand	____________________
thumb	____________________

Write the french translation of each word below.

ENGLISH	FRENCH
pants	_ _ _ _ _ _ _ _ _ _ _ _ _
socks	_ _ _ _ _ _ _ _ _ _ _ _ _
shoes	_ _ _ _ _ _ _ _ _ _ _ _ _
t-shirt	_ _ _ _ _ _ _ _ _ _ _ _ _
underwear	_ _ _ _ _ _ _ _ _ _ _ _ _

Write the french translation of each word below.

ENGLISH	FRENCH
lemon	_ _ _ _ _ _ _ _ _ _ _ _ _
avocado	_ _ _ _ _ _ _ _ _ _ _ _ _
eggplant	_ _ _ _ _ _ _ _ _ _ _ _ _
onion	_ _ _ _ _ _ _ _ _ _ _ _ _
corn	_ _ _ _ _ _ _ _ _ _ _ _ _

Write the english translation of each word below.

FRENCH	ENGLISH
Bonjour	– – – – – – – – – – – – –
Bonsoir	– – – – – – – – – – – – –
À demain	– – – – – – – – – – – – –
Merci beaucoup	– – – – – – – – – – – – –
Salut	– – – – – – – – – – – – –

 **Write the english translation of each word below.**

FRENCH	ENGLISH
langue	_ _ _ _ _ _ _ _ _ _ _ _
cou	_ _ _ _ _ _ _ _ _ _ _ _
sourcil	_ _ _ _ _ _ _ _ _ _ _ _
arrière	_ _ _ _ _ _ _ _ _ _ _ _
nombril	_ _ _ _ _ _ _ _ _ _ _ _

 **Write the english translation of each word below.**

FRENCH	ENGLISH
ventre	_ _ _ _ _ _ _ _ _ _ _ _ _ _ _
jambe	_ _ _ _ _ _ _ _ _ _ _ _ _ _ _
bras	_ _ _ _ _ _ _ _ _ _ _ _ _ _ _
pied	_ _ _ _ _ _ _ _ _ _ _ _ _ _ _
poitrine	_ _ _ _ _ _ _ _ _ _ _ _ _ _ _

Write the english translation of each word below.

FRENCH	ENGLISH
une casquette	_ _ _ _ _ _ _ _ _ _ _ _ _
un pantalon	_ _ _ _ _ _ _ _ _ _ _ _ _
une jupe	_ _ _ _ _ _ _ _ _ _ _ _ _
des chaussures	_ _ _ _ _ _ _ _ _ _ _ _ _
des chaussettes	_ _ _ _ _ _ _ _ _ _ _ _ _

Write the english translation of each word below.

FRENCH	ENGLISH
citrouille	– – – – – – – – – – – – –
poivron	– – – – – – – – – – – – –
les raisins	– – – – – – – – – – – – –
poire	– – – – – – – – – – – – –
pomme	– – – – – – – – – – – – –

Answers!

EXERCISE 1

ENGLISH	FRENCH
Good night	Bonne nuit
Hello	Bonsoir
Thank you	Merci
Good luck	Bonne chance
Welcome	Bienvenue

EXERCISE 2

ENGLISH	FRENCH
face	visage
nose	nez
hair	cheveux
eye	œil
teeth	les dents

EXERCISE 3

ENGLISH	FRENCH
ear	oreille
head	tête
chin	menton
hand	main
thumb	pouce

EXERCISE 4

ENGLISH	FRENCH
pants	un pantalon
socks	des chaussettes
shoes	des chaussures
t-shirt	un tee-shirt
underwear	Un slip

EXERCISE 5

ENGLISH	FRENCH
lemon	citron
avocado	avocat
eggplant	aubergine
onion	oignon
corn	blé

EXERCISE 6

FRENCH	ENGLISH
Bonjour	Hello
Bonsoir	Hello (after 7pm)
À demain	See you tomorrow
Merci beaucoup	Thank you very much
Salut	Hi / Bye

EXERCISE 7

FRENCH	ENGLISH
langue	tongue
cou	neck
sourcil	eyebrow
arrière	back
nombril	belly button

EXERCISE 8

FRENCH	ENGLISH
ventre	belly
jambe	leg
bras	arm
pied	foot
poitrine	chest

EXERCISE 9

FRENCH	ENGLISH
une casquette	a cap
un pantalon	pants
une jupe	a skirt
des chaussures	shoes
des chaussettes	socks

EXERCISE 10

FRENCH	ENGLISH
citrouille	pumpkin
poivron	bell pepper
les raisins	grapes
poire	pear
pomme	apple

Visit

www.BabyProfessorBooks.com

to download Free Baby Professor eBooks
and view our catalog of new and exciting
Children's Books

www.ingramcontent.com/pod-product-compliance
Lightning Source LLC
Chambersburg PA
CBHW060224120726
48009CB00003B/139